MW01114454

This notebook belongs to:

....

Published by HAB Publication

Made in the USA
Middletown, DE
22 November 2022

15765017R00068